The Renal Diet

COOKBOOK & GUIDE

vigor&belle

© 2016

Follow us in Social Media!

Connect with other people, get the latest info, discuss the most recent vigor&belle products or simply show your love for the vigor&belle brand!

Facebook
Connect and become friends with other fans, or comment, discuss the latest posts and releases from vigor&belle.

Instagram
Follow vigor&belle on Instagram for even more healthy recipes, lifestyle and beauty ideas.

Pinterest
Pin, like and comment your favorite vigor&belle recipes and beauty trends.

TABLE OF CONTENTS

Introduction: What is Kidney Disease?

Kidney disease is a health condition which results in the kidneys not working properly. This condition can be spotted quite early on through a variety of blood and urine tests.

What are the symptoms of kidney disease?

The symptoms of kidney disease can include:

- Insomnia
- Shortness of breath
- Nausea
- Blood in the urine
- Protein in the urine
- Swollen ankles, hands, or feet
- Erectile dysfunction
- Muscle cramps
- Itchy skin
- Poor appetite
- Weight loss

If you have a few or many of the above symptoms, you may not necessarily have kidney disease. The above symptoms are often present in other conditions too. If you are concerned about any of your symptoms, please speak to your doctor.

What causes kidney disease?

More often than not, kidney disease is caused by another condition or conditions that can strain the kidneys. Some of the most causes of this disease can be diabetes, and high blood pressure.

It's thought that as many as 25 % of all cases are as a result of high blood pressure. Diabetes is thought to be responsible for just under 25% of cases of kidney disease.

The other conditions often associated with kidney disease include:

- Inflammation of the kidney (Glomerulonephritis)
- Kidney stones
- A kidney infection (Pyelonephritis)
- Prostate disease
- Polycystic kidney disease
- Systematic lupus erythematosus
- Abnormal kidney development in an unborn baby

All of the above conditions are likely to cause kidney disease, or indeed be a major factor in the development of the condition.

If you are concerned about any of your symptoms, or you're worried that you may develop kidney disease, please speak to your doctor.

What is the Renal Diet?

The renal diet is a type of diet that has been specifically designed to help those who have kidney disease. This diet is unlike many other diets as it often contains a specific number of nutrients that are vital at helping to keep your kidney as healthy as possible.

How does the renal diet work?

The renal diet works by paying close attention to the amount of sodium, potassium and phosphorus you consume at each and every meal. It's these three nutrients that can help you to stay as healthy as you can, while doing your best to fight kidney disease.

How can this diet improve your health?

The renal diet can help you to improve your health because it asks you to reduce the amount of salt you consume. Reducing your salt (Sodium) intake can help you to control the disease, and therefore improve your condition or simply prevent it from getting any worse.

Here are a few tips that can help you to reduce your salt (Sodium intake):

- Don't add salt to your food
- If you're cooking meals from scratch, don't add salt
- When shopping for pre-packaged food, always choose the 'No added salt' option.

- Stay away from meats that tend to contain a lot of salt (Bacon, chicken nuggets, canned soup, hot dogs, sausages)
- Always read the labels, some foods you buy may contain a lot of salt. You may have to switch your brand, or stop eating the product all together if it contains too much salt.

Phosphorus

Phosphorus can build up in your kidneys if they fail to work properly. Too much phosphorus can result in the calcium being removed from your bones, before collecting in your blood vessels, or even your skin. This process can lead to bone disease.

- Limit the amount of dairy milk you drink to no more than 1 cup a day
- Avoid beer
- Avoid whole grain bread and crackers. White bread is ok
- Cheese should be limited to 1 ounce per day
- Yogurt should be limited to 1 ounce per day
- Many sodas contain phosphorus, but clear ones are likely to contain very little. It may be easier to avoid sodas completely.
- Broccoli, Brussels sprouts, and mushrooms should be eaten no more than once a week, and have no more than 1 cup at a time.

Potassium

Potassium helps the muscles to work, and it's this nutrient that can build up in your blood if you have an issue with your kidneys. You should also be aware that too much potassium can even affect your heart. The good news is that this mineral is usually only found in:

- Oranges, grapefruits and juices made from these fruits
- Tomatoes, tomato sauce, and tomato juice
- Bananas, pumpkins, melons (Except watermelon)
- Winter squashes, Swiss chard, spinach, cooked greens, collards and kale
- Prune juice, dried beans.
- Granola, salt substitutes, bran cereals

Potatoes can contain a lot of potassium, but the trick is to boil them for 10 minutes, and drain the water away. Use fresh water, and boil them again, before draining the water away. You can boil them a third time if you so wish.

The next chapter is the first of many that guide you through a wide range of meal ideas. The meals contained in this book are thought to be suitable for those who are taking part in the renal diet.

Substitutions

If you read through the recipes and discover that one recipe asks for sugar, please be aware you can substitute with a low-carb sweetener. You can also find low calorie egg substitutes if you're concerned about cholesterol.

Please note I have not kept a close eye on your potassium/sodium levels each day. If you wish to adjust the amounts you consume in one day, please do so accordingly. The recipes contained in this book can be adjusted to meet your needs, and tastes.

Day 1 of Healing Meal Plan

Breakfast

<u>Apple and Onion Omelet</u>
Serves: 2

<u>Ingredients:</u>
3 eggs (Large, beaten)
2 tbsp cheddar (Shredded)
¼ cup milk (Low fat)
1 apple (Peeled, cored, sliced thinly)
1 tbsp water
¾ cup onion (Sweet, sliced thinly)
Sprinkle black pepper
1 tbsp butter

<u>Method</u>
Preheat your oven to 400 Fahrenheit, and combine the milk, pepper, water and eggs together, and beat well. Set to one side.

Add the butter to a skillet on a medium heat, and heat until melted. The add the apple and onion, and sauté until the onion is clear.

Now evenly spread the apple and onion out, and sprinkle the cheese over the top. Take the egg mix, and pour it over the cheese. Cook the omelet on a medium heat until it starts to set at the edges.

Now place the skillet in the oven, and cook until the omelet is set (For about 10 minutes). Serve.

Nutrients per serving:
Protein: 13 g
Carbs: 22
Fat: 16 g
Cholesterol: 303 mg
Potassium: 341 mg
Sodium: 169 mg
Phosphorus: 238 mg

Lunch

Beef & Barley Soup
Serves: 5

Ingredients:
1 pound beef stew meat (Diced)
¼ cup barley
2 tbsp vegetable oil
1 potato (Diced)
½ cup onion (Chopped)
8 ounces package vegetables (Frozen)
¼ cup mushrooms (Sliced)
1 ½ cups water
¼ tsp garlic (Minced)
7 ounces low sodium chicken broth
Pinch thyme
Pepper to season

Method
Season the beef with the pepper, and then add half of the vegetable oil to a stew pot. Heat the oil slightly, and add the beef to the pot. Sauté for five minutes, and add the rest of the oil. Now add the mushrooms, carrots and onions to the pot along with the vegetables, barley and potatoes. Stir well, and allow the soup to boil. As soon as the soup starts boiling,

cover, and reduce the heat. Simmer for about 1- ½ hours. Serve.

Nutrients per serving:
Protein: 23 g
Carbs: 22 g
Potassium: 678 mg
Sodium: 105 mg
Phosphorus: 250 mg

Dinner

Mexican Chicken Pizza
Serves: 4

Ingredients:
4 flour tortillas
½ cup Monterey Jack cheese (Shredded)
Cooking spray
2 tbsp lime juice
1 cup whole kernel corn (No salt)
1 clove garlic (Chopped)
¼ cup onion (Chopped)
2 cups roasted chicken breast (Chopped)
½ cup red bell peppers (Chopped)
4 tsp cilantro (Chopped)

Method
Preheat your oven to 350 Fahrenheit, and add the tortillas to a baking sheet that's been sprayed with the cooking spray. Bake for about 10 minutes, or until the tortillas are starting to turn a little brown. Once they're done, place one tortilla on a plate, and the other 3 on top of it, and press down in order to flatten them.

Heat a skillet on a medium-high heat, and add some cooking spray. Add the corn, and cook for about 1 minute, or until the corn is looking a little burned. Now add the chicken, onion, garlic and red peppers, and cook until they're heated through (This should take a few minutes). Once the ingredients are heated, remove them from the heat, and then add the lime juice.

Take the tortillas, and add them to another baking sheet, and divide the chicken mix between them. Add the cheese on top, and place the tortillas in the oven for a few minutes, or until the cheese is melted. Remove from the oven, and sprinkle the cilantro over the cheese. Serve.

Nutrients per serving:
Protein: 26 g
Carbs: 31 g
Fat: 9 g
Cholesterol: 59 mg
Potassium: 329 mg
Sodium: 253 mg
Phosphorus: 250 mg

Phos 738
Sodium 527
Potassium 1348

Day 2 of Healing Meal Plan

Breakfast

Plain pancakes
Makes 12-15

Ingredients:
3 eggs
3 tbsp butter (Melted)
1 1/3 cups milk
¾ cup all-purpose flour

Method
Add the milk and eggs to a blender, and blend well.

Now add the flour a little at a time, and blend for 60 seconds before covering and allowing to stand for one hour.

Once the hour is up, pour the batter into a large bowl, and add the melted butter, whisk well. Place a skillet on a medium-high heat, and add some cooking spray to the pan. Now take ¼ cup of batter, and pour it into the skillet. Ensure the batter reaches the edges of the pan, and allow the mixture to bubble. Once the pancake is golden on one side, remove from the skillet, and fold it in half, place on a plate, and do the same with the rest of the batter. Serve.

Nutrients per serving (1 pancake):
Protein: 3 g
Carbs: 6 g
Fat: 3 g
Cholesterol: 46 mg

Potassium: 50 mg
Sodium: 29 mg
Phosphorus: 45 mg

Lunch

<u>Chicken & Asparagus Pasta</u>
Serves: 4

<u>Ingredients:</u>
½ pound asparagus spears (Trimmed, diagonally cut)
1/8 cup feta cheese (Crumbled)
4 ounces chicken breast (Skinless, boneless, cubed)
¾ tsp oregano
8 ounces penne pasta (Uncooked)
½ garlic clove (Chopped)
2 ½ tbsp olive oil
¼ cup chicken broth (Low sodium)
Pinch black pepper
Pinch garlic powder

<u>Method</u>
Bring a pot of water to the boil, and add the pasta.
Cook the pasta as per the manufacturer's instructions.
Once the pasta is cooked, drain and place to one side.
Take a skillet and gently heat 1 ½ tbsp olive oil on a
medium-high heat. Add the chicken and stir, then add
the garlic powder and pepper. Stir again. Cook the
chicken thoroughly (This should take 5 minutes).
Once the chicken is done, set to one side. Now add the
chicken broth to the skillet, and stir in the garlic,
oregano, and a little more pepper and garlic powder if
you have it. Cover, and let the mixture steam for 5
minutes, or until the asparagus has turned tender.

Place the chicken back into the skillet, and warm it through. Once the chicken has warmed through, spoon it onto the pasta, and drizzle with the rest of the olive oil. Stir once more, and sprinkle the cheese on top. Serve.

Nutrients per serving:
Protein: 18 g
Carbs: 49 g
Potassium: 243 mg
Sodium: 110 mg
Phosphorus: 193 mg

Dinner

Cheesy Meatloaf
Serves: 6

Ingredients:
1 pound beef (Ground)
1 ounce cheddar cheese (Shredded)
1 egg
1 tbsp onion powder
½ cup bread crumbs
1 tbsp garlic powder
½ cup brown sugar
8 ounce tomato sauce (Low sodium)

Method
Preheat your oven to 350 Fahrenheit. Take a bowl and add the beef, 3 ounces of the tomato sauce, brown sugar, onion powder, garlic powder and half of the bread crumbs. Using your hands, mix the ingredients thoroughly, and then cut them in half. Place one half onto a casserole dish, and sprinkle the cheese on top.

Then take the rest of the mixture, and put it on top of that. Using a spoon or a spatula, flatten down the top of the mixture, and then add the rest of the tomato sauce. Now take the rest of the bread crumbs, and sprinkle them on top.

Place the meatloaf in the oven, and cook for 1 hour. Serve.

Nutrients per serving:
Protein: 19 g
Carbs: 21 g
Fat: 11 g
Cholesterol: 92 mg
Potassium: 397 mg
Sodium: 154 mg
Phosphorus: 186 mg

Day 3 of Healing Meal Plan

Breakfast

Egg and Chorizo Tortilla
Serves: 1

Ingredients:
1/3 cup chorizo (Chopped)
1 tortilla
1 egg

Method
Add the chorizo to a skillet and cook on a medium heat until the meat is cooked through, this should take 5 minutes. Drain away any fat, and then add the egg to the skillet. Stir well to combine. Once the eggs are cooked and is nicely mixed with the chorizo, spoon the mixture into the tortilla, and serve.

Nutrients per serving:
Protein: 16 g
Carbs: 15 g
Fat: 11 g
Cholesterol: 211 mg
Potassium: 284 mg
Sodium: 317 mg
Phosphorus: 82 mg

Lunch

Cornbread Salad
Serves: 6

Ingredients:
6 cups iceberg lettuce (Shredded)
¾ tsp dry Ranch dressing mixture
½ cup bell pepper (Chopped)
2 tbsp mayonnaise
½ cup radishes (Sliced)
½ cup sour cream
½ cup cucumber (Peeled, diced)
2 cups corn bread (Fried, crumbled)
½ cup cilantro

Method
Add the lettuce, radishes, pepper, cucumber, and cilantro to a bow, and combine well. Now add the corn bread, and mix well. In another bowl, add the mayonnaise, ranch dressing, and sour cream, and mix well. Pour the mayonnaise mix over the salad, and stir well. Place the salad in the refrigerator for at least 30 minutes. Serve.

Nutrients per serving:
Protein: 4 g
Carbs: 25 g
Fat: 11 g
Cholesterol: 29 mg
Potassium: 231 mg
Sodium: 175 mg
Phosphorus: 71 mg

Dinner

Chicken & Broccoli Casserole
Serves: 6

Ingredients:
2 cups broccoli (Cooked)

¼ cup Parmesan (Shredded)
1 onion (Chopped)
2 cups cheddar (Shredded)
2 chicken breasts (Diced)
2 cups rice (Cooked)
2 tbsp margarine
2 cups milk
2 eggs (Beaten)

Method
Add the onion to a pan, and cook until it's browned. Now add the chicken and margarine, and cook for about 10 minutes on a medium heat. Place the remaining ingredients apart from the Parmesan into a casserole dish, and mix well. Add the chicken and onion to the casserole dish, mix again. Sprinkle the Parmesan on top, and cook at 350 Fahrenheit for about 1 ¼ hours. Serve.

Nutrients per serving:
Protein: 26 g
Carbs: 26 g
Potassium: 371 mg
Sodium: 388 mg
Phosphorus: 243 mg

Day 4 of Healing Meal Plan

Breakfast

<u>Crunchy French Toast</u>
Serves: 3

<u>Ingredients:</u>
2 eggs
1 ½ tbsp cinnamon
1 tbsp sugar
1 tbsp margarine (Unsalted)
1/3 cup non-dairy liquid creamer
¾ cup cornflakes (Crushed)
½ tsp vanilla extract
3 slices white bread

<u>Method</u>
Add the eggs, creamer, vanilla, and sugar to a pie pan, and place the bread in too. Let the bread soak in the egg mix for about 5 minutes, or until it has turned soft. Turn the bread over, and let it soak on the other side.

Take a shallow dish and add the cornflakes, spreading them evenly along the bottom. Once the bread is soaked, remove it from the pan, and place it on top of the cornflakes, push each slice of bread down on the cornflakes softly so they stick. Turn each slice of bread over, and repeat on the other side.

Take a skillet, and melt the margarine, before adding the slices of bread to the skillet. Cook on a medium-high heat, and allow to brown on each side. When the toast is done, add the cinnamon and sugar to a bowl, mix well, and sprinkle it over the slices of toast. Serve.

Nutrients per serving:
Protein: 6 g
Carbs: 29 g
Fat: 12 g
Cholesterol: 125 g
Potassium: 374 mg
Sodium: 244 mg
Phosphorus: 82

Lunch

Potato Soup
Serves: 2-3

Ingredients:
1 large potato (Baked)
¼ cup sour cream (Fat free)
1/6 cup flour
2 ounces Monterey Jack cheese (Shredded)
2 cups skim milk
¼ tsp pepper

Method
Cut the potato length-wise, and scoop out the middle. Now add the flour to a large pan, and then pour in the milk a little at a time. Stir well, until the flour and milk have thoroughly combined. Add the pepper and the scooped out bits of potato to the pan, and stir well. Cook on a medium heat until the sauce is starting to bubble and is nice and thick.

Now add the cheese, and keep stirring until it is melted. Remove the pan from the heat, add the sour cream, and stir well. Serve.

Nutrients per serving:
Protein: 15 g
Carbs: 29 g
Fat: 1 g
Potassium: 594 mg
Sodium: 272 mg
Phosphorus: 326 mg

Dinner

Pork Chops With Orange Glaze
Serves: 4

Ingredients:
1/3 cup orange marmalade
4 pork chops
2 tsp brown mustard (Spicy)
4 tbsp green onions (Chopped)

Method
Add the mustard and marmalade to a pan and stir well. Heat on a medium heat stirring for 2 minutes. Add the onions to a skillet that's been sprayed with cooking spray, and cook them until they are crisp. Add the marmalade, and allow to warm through. Now place the chops in a broiler, and cook them on each side for about 3 minutes. Once the pork chops are done, remove them from the heat, and pour the glaze over them. Serve with your choice of vegetables.

Nutrients per serving:
Protein: 21 g

Carbs: 18 g
Fat: 11 g
Cholesterol: 61 mg
Potassium: 322 mg
Sodium: 87 mg
Phosphorus: 179 mg

Day 5 of Healing Meal Plan

Breakfast

Goats Cheese & Dill Weed Scrambled Eggs
Serves: 1

Ingredients:
2 eggs
1 tsp dill weed
1 tbsp goats cheese (Crumbled)
Sprinkle black pepper

Method
Add the eggs to a bowl and mix them well to scramble them. Now pour the eggs into a skillet and turn the heat up to medium-high. Add the black pepper, goats cheese, and dill weed, stir, and cook until the eggs are cooked to your satisfaction. Serve.

Nutrients per serving:
Protein: 16 g
Carbs: 1 g
Fat: 14 g
Cholesterol: 434 mg
Potassium: 192 mg
Sodium: 213 mg
Phosphorus: 250 mg

Lunch

Tiny Turkey Wraps
Serves: 2

Ingredients:
1 red pepper (Roasted, cut into strips)
6 tooth picks
3 tbsp cream cheese (Whipped)
1 tortilla wrap
2 ounces deli turkey (Sliced)
1 cup salad greens

Method
Spread the cheese onto the tortilla, and add the salad greens and turkey. Add the pepper, but space it out evenly. Now roll the tortilla, once it's completely rolled, hold it closed with the tooth picks making sure you space them out evenly. Cut the tortilla into 6 pieces, and serve.

Nutrients per serving:
Protein: 9 g
Carbs: 14 g
Fat: 9 g
Cholesterol: 30 mg
Potassium: 270 mg
Sodium: 440 mg
Phosphorus: 119 mg

Dinner

Green Chili Casserole
Serves: 6

Ingredients:
½ cup all-purpose flour
6 tbsp sour cream
1 tbsp garlic powder
¼ cup cilantro (Chopped)

1 tsp black pepper
¾ cup iceberg lettuce (Chopped)
1 pound pork chops (Cubed)
6 flour tortillas
1 tbsp olive oil
14 ounces chicken broth (Low sodium)
8 ounces green chili peppers (Diced)
1 clove garlic (Minced)

Method

Add the flour, black pepper, pork chops and garlic powder to a zip lock bag, and shake them well. Ensure the pork is coated in flour. Now take a skillet, and heat the oil in it, once the oil is hot, add the pork. Cook the pork thoroughly, and then add it to a slow cooker along with the broth, peppers and garlic. Cook on a low heat for 10 hours. Once 10 hours is up, divide the stew between the tortillas and roll them up. Add the cilantro and lettuce, and then add 1 tbsp of the cream to the top of the tortilla. Serve.

Nutrients per serving:

Protein: 25 g
Carbs: 44 g
Fat: 16 g
Cholesterol: 45 mg
Potassium: 454 mg
Sodium: 552 mg
Phosphorus: 323 mg

Day 6 of Healing Meal Plan

Breakfast

Cheese & Bacon Stuffed Biscuits
Makes 12

Ingredients:
2 cups flour
4 eggs (Scrambled)
¾ cup milk
1 tbsp sugar
1 cup cheddar
8 tbsp butter (Softened, chopped into small pieces)
½ tsp baking soda
¼ cup scallions (Thinly sliced)
1 tbsp lemon juice
¾ cup bacon (Crispy, chopped)

Method
Preheat your oven to 425 Fahrenheit, and then add the flour, sugar butter, baking soda and lemon juice to a bowl. Create a well in the center of the bowl, and add the milk, then knead the mixture so the milk combines nicely.

Now add the eggs, bacon, scallions and cheese, placing them on top and in the center of the mixture. Take opposite edges of the mix and fold it over the eggs, bacon etc. and close it so the egg mix looks like it has a blanket wrapped around it. Place the stuffed biscuits into the oven, and cook for about 10 minutes, or until they are nicely brown. Serve.

Nutrients per serving: (1 biscuit)
Protein: 9 g
Carbs: 19 g
Fat: 21 g
Cholesterol: 106 g
Potassium: 122 mg
Sodium: 235 mg
Phosphorus: 147 mg

Lunch

Cucumber & Mint Salad
Serves: 4

Ingredients:
1 cucumber (Diced)
¼ tsp garlic powder
1 tsp olive oil
¼ tsp black pepper
1 tbsp mint

Method
Add the cucumber, mint, pepper, garlic, and olive oil to a bowl, stir well to combine. Place the salad in the refrigerator to cool for at least 30 minutes. Serve.

Nutrients per serving:
Protein: 1 g
Carbs: 3 g
Fat: 1 g
Cholesterol: 0 mg
Potassium: 122 mg
Sodium: 3 mg
Phosphorus: 20 mg

Dinner

<u>Chicken Lasagna</u>
Serves: 6

<u>Ingredients:</u>
6 ounces chicken breast
1 package lasagna noodles
12 ounces chicken broth (Low sodium)
1 ½ zucchini (Cut length-wise, and then in half)
¼ cup olive oil
½ cup Parmesan (Shredded)
1 onion (Diced)
¼ tsp nutmeg
1 tbsp oregano
1 ½ cup non-dairy creamer
¼ tsp black pepper
6 ounces cream cheese
½ cup mushrooms (Sliced)
3 tbsp flour

<u>Method</u>
Preheat your oven to 375 Fahrenheit. Add the chicken and broth to a pot and allow to boil. The reduce the heat, and allow the chicken to cook thoroughly. Take a sauté pan, and add the olive oil, oregano, onion and black pepper. Sauté for about 5 minutes, or until the onion is soft.

Now add the mushrooms and then take the flour and sprinkle it over the pan evenly. Cook for about 3 minutes, and then add the cream cheese, stirring until the cheese has melted. Add the creamer to the pan, and stir once more.

Once the mix has started to thicken add the nutmeg, and the Parmesan, and stir for 5 minutes. Now take the chicken from the pot, but leave the broth in there. Shred the chicken, and then put it to one side. Add the broth to the cream mix, and stir while it heats for 2 minutes.

Now it's time to add a lasagna noodle to the pan. Pour about 1/3 of the sauce over the noodle, and then add about ½ of the chicken. Place ½ of the zucchini on top, and then repeat until you've used up all the ingredients. You should finish your lasagna with a layer of sauce.

Place the lasagna in the oven covered in foil, and cook for about 30 minutes. Remove the foil, and cook for a few more minutes. Serve.

Nutrients per serving:
Protein:
Carbs: 32 g
Potassium: 317 mg
Sodium: 277 mg
Phosphorus: 179 mg

Day 7 of Healing Meal Plan

Breakfast

Cheese & Tomato Lemon Pepper Bagel
Serves: 2

Ingredients:
1 bagel
1 tsp lemon pepper seasoning (Low sodium)
2 tbsp cream cheese
2 slices red onion
2 slices tomato

Method
Slice the bagel, and then toast it until it's done to your satisfaction. Add the cream cheese, and spread well. Add the onion and tomato slices. Sprinkle with the lemon pepper, and serve.

Nutrients per serving:
Protein: 5 g
Carbs: 19 g
Fat: 6 g
Cholesterol: 15 mg
Potassium: 162 mg
Sodium: 219 mg
Phosphorus: 50 mg

Lunch

Chicken & Corn Chowder
Serves: 6

Ingredients:
6 slices bacon
2 cups mocha mix
4 green onions (Chopped)
3 tbsp thyme
1 onion (Chopped)
4 chicken breasts (Boneless, chopped)
3 ½ cups low sodium chicken broth
4 cups corn
2 potatoes (Diced)

Method
Cook the bacon until it's nice and crispy, remove the bacon from the pan, but leave the fat in. Add the onions to the same pan, and sauté them until they're clear. Add the potatoes and broth, and place a lid on the pan. Simmer for about 10 minutes, and then add the chicken, corn, and thyme. Cover again, and cook for another 15 minutes, or until the chicken is done. Once the chicken is done, add the cream, stir, and simmer for 2 minutes. Now add the bacon, green onions and pepper, and stir. Serve.

Nutrients per serving:
Protein: 31 g
Carbs: 55 g
Fat: 6 g
Potassium: 1172 mg
Sodium: 260 mg
Phosphorus: 438 mg

Dinner

Baked Trout
Serves: 4

Ingredients:
1 pound rainbow trout fillet (Washed, dried)
¼ tsp paprika
½ tbsp cooking oil
½ tsp lemon pepper (No salt added)
¼ tsp salt

Method
Preheat your oven to 350 Fahrenheit, and rub the trout gently with a bit of oil. Now place the fillets in a baking dish with the skin facing downwards. Add all of the seasonings to a bowl and stir well. Sprinkle the seasoning mix over the fillets. Add the trout to the oven, and bake for about 30 minutes, or until it can easily be flaked with a fork. Serve with your choice of vegetables.

Nutrients per serving:
Protein: 21 g
Carbs: 0 g
Fat: 8 g
Cholesterol: 58 mg
Potassium: 385 mg
Sodium: 169 mg
Phosphorus: 227 mg

Day 8 of Healing Meal Plan

Breakfast

Blueberry Smoothie
Serves: 3

Ingredients:
1 ¼ cup pineapple juice
½ cup water
2 cups blueberries (Frozen)
2 tsp sugar
¾ cup egg whites (Pasteurized)

Method
Add all of the ingredients to a blender or juicer and blend well. Serve.

Nutrients per serving:
Protein: 7.5 g
Carbs: 31 g
Fat: 3 g
Potassium: 290 mg
Sodium: 104.1 mg
Phosphorus: 27.5 mg

Lunch

Beef Pita Pocket
Serves: 3

Ingredients:
1 tbsp olive oil
3 white pita breads
½ onion (Sliced)

¼ tsp black pepper
1 cup mushrooms (Sliced)
½ tbsp browning sauce
½ red bell pepper
½ tbsp Worcestershire sauce
¼ cup parsley (Chopped)
½ pound ground beef

Method
Heat the oil in a skillet, and add the bell pepper, onion, and mushrooms, Sauté for about 5 minutes, or until tender, and then set to one side. Place the beef in the skillet, and cook for about 5 minutes, and remove any fat. Add the browning sauce and Worcestershire sauce along with the black pepper, and cook for a few more minutes.

Now add the vegetables and stir them well. Add the parsley, stir again, and cook until it has heated through. Remove the skillet from the heat, and set to one side. Take the pitas and warm them, before opening them up and filling with the beef mix. Serve.

Nutrients per serving:
Protein: 21 g
Carbs: 37 g
Fat: 21 g
Cholesterol: 57 mg
Potassium: 443 mg
Sodium: 393 mg
Phosphorus: 193 mg

Dinner

Beef & Turkey Chili
Serves: 6

Ingredients:
1 pound ground turkey
4 ½ cups white rice (Cooked)
½ pound ground beef
3 ounces tomato paste (Low sodium)
½ onion (Chopped)
1/8 cup chili powder
¼ green bell pepper (Chopped)
1 ½ cups boiling water
1 garlic clove (Chopped)
½ tbsp all-purpose flour
¾ tbsp cumin seeds
¼ tsp paprika
½ tsp oregano
½ tsp salt

Method
Add the beef and turkey to a skillet, and sauté on a medium heat until they are cooked through and brown. Now add the garlic, onion and green pepper, and stir well. Add the paprika, oregano, pepper, salt and cumin, and stir again.

Take the flour, and sprinkle it evenly over the ingredients. Take the boiling water and add the chili powder to it, stir well, and then pour it into the skillet. Stir well. Allow the chili to cook at 1 hour on a medium-low heat. Once the hour is up, add the tomato paste, stir, and then remove any grease from the surface. Cook for another 30 minutes. Take the rice, divide it between 4 plates, and then spoon the chili over it. Serve.

Nutrients per serving:
Protein: 27 g
Carbs: 38 g
Fat: 14 g
Cholesterol: 75 mg
Potassium: 552 mg
Sodium: 300 mg
Phosphorus: 278 mg

Day 9 of Healing Meal Plan

Breakfast

Multi-Grain Hot Oat Cereal
Serves: 2

Ingredients:
1 ¾ cups water
3 tbsp couscous (Uncooked)
2 tbsp grits (Uncooked)
1 tbsp oats (Uncooked)
1 tbsp bulgar wheat (Uncooked)
1 tbsp roasted whole buckwheat (Uncooked)

Method
Add the water to a pot and allow it to boil. Once the
water is boiling add the grits and stir just a little. Now
add the oats, bulgar, and buckwheat and stir a little.
Reduce the heat to a good simmer, and spray some
non-stick cooking spray onto the surface of the water.
Cover, and allow to simmer for about 25 minutes.
Once the allotted time is up, remove the pot, and add
the couscous. Allow to stand for 6-8 minutes, and
serve.

Nutrients per serving:
Protein: 5 g
Carbs: 30 g
Fat: 1 g
Cholesterol: 0 mg
Potassium: 87 mg
Sodium: 7 mg
Phosphorus: 91 mg

Lunch

<u>Cranberry Salad</u>
Serves: 2

<u>Ingredients:</u>
2/3 cup cranberries
1 cup mixed salad leaves
1/6 cup sugar
1/3 cup pineapple chunks (Diced)

<u>Method</u>
Add the cranberries to a food processor, along with the sugar, and blend until smooth. Let the cranberry mix stand for a few minutes before adding the pineapple, Stir well, and then fold the mixed salad leaves in. Place in the refrigerator for at least 30 minutes, and serve.

<u>Nutrients per serving:</u>
Protein: 0 g
Carbs: 18 g
Fat: 1 g
Cholesterol: 3 mg
Potassium: 43 mg
Sodium: 9 mg
Phosphorus: 7 mg

Dinner

<u>Apple And Pork Roast</u>
Serves: 4-5

Ingredients:
1 apple (Cored, cut into wedges)
½ cup apple sauce (Unsweetened)
½ red onion (Chopped)
Sprinkle black pepper
Sprinkle cinnamon
Sprinkle salt
1 ½ pound pork roast

Method
Add the apple to a slow cooker along with the onion.
Add about 1/3 of the cinnamon. Take the salt and
pepper, and rub it gently onto the pork. Add the pork
to the slow cooker, and pour the apple sauce over it.
Now add the rest of the cinnamon on top, and cook on
a high heat for 2-3 hours, or until the pork is done.
Serve.

Nutrients per serving:
Protein: 32 g
Carbs: 8 g
Fat: 10 g
Cholesterol: 90 mg
Potassium: 486 mg
Sodium: 140 mg
Phosphorus: 256 mg

Day 10 of Healing Meal Plan

Breakfast

Chili & Salsa Breakfast Burrito
Serves: 2

Ingredients:
4 eggs
2 tbsp salsa
3 tbsp green chilies (Diced)
2 tortillas
½ tsp hot pepper sauce
¼ tsp cumin

Method
Add the chilies and eggs to a bowl and beat them together. Then add the hot sauce and cumin, and stir well. Add the egg mix to a skillet that's been sprayed with cooking spray, and cook on a medium heat for about 2 minutes, or until the eggs are done to your satisfaction.

Heat the tortillas for 20 seconds in a microwave, and then spoon half of the egg mix into the center each tortilla. Roll the tortilla up, place it on a plate and add the salsa to the side. Serve.

Nutrients per serving:
Protein: 15 g
Carbs: 20 g
Fat: 12 g
Potassium: 246 mg
Sodium: 384 mg
Phosphorus: 184 mg

Lunch

Apple & Rice Salad
Serves: 5

Ingredients:
2 cups rice (Cooked and chilled)
1 garlic clove (Minced)
2 cups apples (Chopped)
2 tsp orange peel (Shredded)
½ cup celery (Sliced)
2 tbsp Dijon mustard
2 tbsp sunflower seeds (Shelled)
2 tsp honey
2 tbsp balsamic vinegar
1 tbsp olive oil

Method
Add the apple, rice, sunflower seeds, and celery to a bowl. Now take another bowl, and add the rest of the ingredients, and stir well. Pour this mixture over the rice bowl, and stir well to coat. Serve.

Nutrients per serving:
Protein: 5 g
Carbs: 59 g
Fat: 2 g
Potassium: 180 mg
Sodium: 31 mg
Phosphorus: 100 mg

Dinner

<u>Shrimp Quesadilla</u>
Serves: 2

<u>Ingredients:</u>
5 ounces shrimp (Uncooked, shelled, deveined, chopped)
2 tbsp Jalapeño cheddar (Shredded)
2 tbsp cilantro (Chopped)
4 tsp salsa
1 tbsp lemon juice
2 tbsp sour cream
¼ tsp cumin
2 flour tortillas (Burrito size)
1/8 tsp cayenne pepper

<u>Method</u>
Add the lemon juice, cilantro, cayenne pepper and cumin to a zip lock bag. Add the shrimp to the bag, and shake it well so the shrimp is covered in the marinade. Allow to stand for 5 minutes. Now heat a skillet on a medium heat, and add the shrimp along with the marinade. Fry for 2 minutes, stirring constantly until the shrimp has turned orange. Take the skillet off the heat, remove the shrimp, but keep the marinade there.

Add the cream to the skillet and stir well.

Now heat the tortillas, and add 2 tsp of the salsa to each tortilla. Add half of the shrimp mix and 1 tbsp cheese to each tortilla. Place 1 tbsp of sour cream on top of each tortilla, and then fold the tortilla in half. Add a tortilla to the skillet so that it heats, then remove it. Repeat with the other tortilla, and then cut them both into quarters. Sprinkle the cilantro on top, and serve.

Nutrients per serving:
Protein: 20 g
Carbs: 26 g
Fat: 15 g
Cholesterol: 118 mg
Potassium: 276 mg
Sodium: 398 mg
Phosphorus: 243 mg

Day 11 of Healing Meal Plan

Breakfast

<u>Apple & Cinnamon French Toast</u>
Serves: 4-5

<u>Ingredients:</u>
1/3 cup brown sugar
½ tbsp vanilla
¼ cup butter (Unsalted, melted)
¾ cup un-enriched rice milk
1 ½ tsp cinnamon
3 eggs
2 tart apples (The biggest you can find, peeled, cored, chopped)
Italian bread (½ pound, chopped)
¼ cup sweetened cranberries (Dried)

<u>Method</u>
Add the butter, sugar, and 1/3 of the cinnamon to a baking dish. Stir well, and spread the mix evenly on the bottom of the dish. Now add the apples & cranberries on top of the butter mix. Add the bread on top of the apples.

Take the rice milk, eggs, remaining cinnamon, and vanilla, and mix together in a bowl. Now pour the mixture over the bread so that it completely covers it. Cover the mixture, and place it in your refrigerator for up to 24 hours (Minimum of 4). Once the allotted time has passed, preheat your oven to 375 Fahrenheit, and cook the mixture for about 30 minutes with the lid on. Remove the lid, and cook for another 10-15 minutes, or until the mixture is bubbling. Once the apple & cinnamon mix is done, remove it from the oven, and allow to stand for 5 minutes. Sprinkle with sugar if you wish, and serve.

Nutrients per serving:
Protein: 9 g
Carbs: 63 g
Fat: 16 g
Cholesterol: 151 g
Potassium: 210 mg
Sodium: 380 mg
Phosphorus: 136 mg

Lunch

Fruity Chicken Curry Salad
Serves: 4

Ingredients:
2 chicken breasts (Cooked, skinned, boneless, diced)
1/3 cup mayonnaise
½ celery stalk (Chopped)
¼ tsp curry powder
¼ cup onion (Chopped)
Sprinkle black pepper
½ apple (Chopped)
¼ cup water chestnuts (Chopped)
4 red grapes (Seedless)
4 green grapes (Seedless)

Method
Add all of the ingredients to a bowl, and toss to combine. Serve.

Nutrients per serving:
Protein: 14 g
Carbs: 6 g
Fat: 18 g
Cholesterol: 44 mg
Potassium: 200 mg
Sodium: 162 mg
Phosphorus: 115 mg

Dinner

Ravioli With Zucchini
Serves: 4

Ingredients:
9 ounces beef ravioli (Frozen)
¼ cup low sodium chicken broth
2 cups zucchini (Chopped)
1/8 tsp black pepper
3 green onions (Chopped)
½ tsp dried cilantro
1 red bell pepper (Chopped)
½ tsp garlic powder

Method
Cook the ravioli as per the manufacturer's instructions. Now add some cooking spray to a skillet, and turn it up to a medium-high heat. Add the bell pepper, cilantro, zucchini, black pepper and green onions. Cook for about 5 minutes, or until the vegetables are crispy.

Once the ravioli is done, drain away any excess liquid, and then add the broth. Stir well, and add this to the vegetables, and stir again. Cover the skillet, and cook the ravioli on a low heat for about 5-7 minutes, or until it's heated through. Stir gently, and serve.

Nutrients per serving:
Protein: 12 g
Carbs: 27 g
Fat: 9 g
Cholesterol: 57 mg
Potassium: 405 mg
Sodium: 258 mg
Phosphorus: 155 mg

Day 12 of Healing Meal Plan

Breakfast

<u>Waffles</u>
Serves: 4

<u>Ingredients:</u>
¼ cup water (Warm)
1 egg (Lightly beaten)
1 envelope dry yeast
½ cup cornmeal
1 cup un-enriched rice drink
¾ cup white flour
1/8 cup canola
½ tsp sugar
Sprinkle salt

<u>Method</u>
Add the yeast and water to a bowl, stir, and let the yeast dissolve. Allow to stand for 5 minutes, and add the oil, sugar, rice drink, and salt. Now add the cornmeal, flour, and eggs, and stir, but not too much.

Place the mixture in a warm place for 15 minutes, and allow it to rise. Once risen, add to a waffle iron and cook as per the manufacturer's instructions. Serve.

<u>Nutrients per serving:</u>
Protein: 5 g
Carbs: 30 g
Fat: 9 g
Cholesterol: 53 mg
Potassium: 109 mg
Sodium: 78 mg

Phosphorus: 96 mg

Lunch

__Hawaiian Style Chicken Sandwich__
Serves: 4

Ingredients:
2 cups chicken (Cooked, diced)
4 flat bread pieces
1 cup pineapple tidbits
½ tsp black pepper
½ cup mayonnaise (Low fat)
½ cup carrots (Shredded)
½ cup green bell pepper (Chopped)

Method
Add all of the ingredients apart from the flat bread pieces to a bowl, and place them in a refrigerator for at least 30 minutes. Once they are nicely chilled, remove and spoon onto the flat breads. Serve.

Nutrients per serving:
Protein: 22 g
Carbs: 24 g
Fat: 17 g
Cholesterol: 62 mg
Potassium: 333 mg
Sodium: 398 mg
Phosphorus: 167 mg

Dinner

Italian Meatballs
Serves: 6

Ingredients:
1 ½ pounds ground beef
½ tsp black pepper
2 eggs (Beaten)
½ cup onion (Chopped)
½ cup oat meal flakes
1 tsp dried oregano
3 tbsp Parmesan
½ tbsp garlic powder
½ tbsp olive oil

Method
Preheat your oven to 375 Fahrenheit, and add all of the ingredients to a bowl. Using your hands, roll the ingredients into 1-inch size meat balls. Take a baking sheet, add the meatballs to it, and bake in the oven for about 15 minutes, or until the meatballs are thoroughly cooked.
Serve with your choice of vegetables

Nutrients per serving (2 meatballs):
Protein: 12 g
Carbs: 3 g
Potassium: 203 mg
Sodium: 66 mg
Phosphorus: 99 mg

Day 13 of Healing Meal Plan

Breakfast

Mixed Berry Smoothie
Serves: 1

Ingredients:
2 ounces cold water
6 ½ grams whey protein powder
½ cup frozen mixed berries
1 ice cube

Method
Add all of the ingredients to a blender or smoothie maker, and blend until smooth. Pour into a glass, and serve.

Nutrients per serving:
Protein: 6 g
Carbs: 11 g
Fat: 4 g
Cholesterol: 11 mg
Potassium: 141 mg
Sodium: 15 mg
Phosphorus: 49 mg

Lunch

Shrimp And Lemon Couscous Salad
Serves: 2-3

Ingredients:
1 ½ cups water
½ cup Parmesan (Grated)

1 cup couscous (Uncooked)
1 tbsp olive oil
1 pound shrimp (Cooked)
3 tbsp lemon juice
1 ½ cup red pepper (Diced)
¼ cup chicken broth (Low salt)
¼ cup green onions (Diced)
½ cup cilantro (Chopped)

Method
Boil the water in a pan and add the couscous, then remove the pan from the heat right away. Cover the pan and let it stand for about 5 minutes, or until the water is absorbed. Fluff the couscous up using a fork, and allow it to cool. Take a bowl and add the peppers, couscous, shrimp, cilantro and onions, and mix well.

In another bowl add the oil, broth, pepper, and lemon juice, stir and pour it over the salad. Toss the salad gently until it's coated in the dressing. Sprinkle the salad with the Parmesan, and serve.

Nutrients per serving:
Protein: 26 g
Carbs: 40 g
Potassium: 375 mg
Sodium: 810 mg
Phosphorus: 444 mg

Dinner

Chicken Pot Pie
Serves: 8

Ingredients:
2 pounds chicken breasts (Boneless, skinless)
12 ounces pasta
12 cups water
2 tbsp parsley (Chopped)
½ tsp thyme
1 cup onion (Diced)
¼ tsp black pepper
1 cup celery (Diced)
2 cups potatoes (Peeled, chopped)
1 ½ cups carrot (Sliced)

Method
Add the chicken to a large pan, and then add the water and the herbs apart from the parsley. Let the water boil, and then reduce the heat and simmer for about 45 minutes. Add the potatoes to another pot, and add enough water to cover them. Allow to boil and then remove from the heat. Drain the water away, and add fresh water. Allow to boil again, and cook for about 10 minutes. Drain the water, and then set to one side.

Remove the chicken from the pot, and set to one side. Skim any fat from the surface of the water. Now add the onion, celery and carrots and heat until the water starts to boil. Cook for 5 minutes, and then add the potatoes, pasta and parsley. Cook until the pasta is tender. Shred the chicken into small pieces, then stir it into the potato mix. Allow the chicken to heat through, and serve.

Nutrients per serving:
Protein: 32 g
Carbs: 42 g
Fat: 4 g
Cholesterol: 70 mg
Potassium: 521 mg
Sodium: 118 mg
Phosphorus: 290 mg

Day 14 of Healing Meal Plan

Breakfast

Red Pepper & Mushroom Omelet
Serves: 2

Ingredients:
½ cup mushrooms (Sliced)
¼ tsp black pepper
2 tbsp onion (Chopped)
2 tbsp cream cheese (Whipped)
¼ cup sweet red peppers (Diced)
1 tsp Worcestershire sauce
2 tsp butter
3 eggs (Beaten)

Method
Place 1 tsp of the butter in a skillet on a medium heat. Add the onion and mushrooms, and sauté for about 5 minutes, or until the onion is clear. Add the red pepper, stir, and set to one side.

Now take the remaining butter, and place it in a skillet, melt it and then add the eggs and Worcestershire sauce, and stir. Cook on a medium heat for 5 minutes, or until the eggs are slightly cooked. Add the vegetable mix, and then spoon on the cream cheese. Cook until the eggs are done to your satisfaction. Remove the eggs from the heat, sprinkle with the black pepper, and serve.

Nutrients per serving:
Protein: 11 g
Carbs: 4 g

Fat: 15 g
Cholesterol: 341 mg
Potassium: 228 mg
Sodium: 276 mg
Phosphorus: 167 mg

Lunch

Tuna Salad Bagel
Serves: 1

Ingredients:
½ cup canned tuna
1 lettuce leaf
1 tbsp onion (Chopped)
1 bagel
1 tbsp celery (Chopped)
1 tbsp mayonnaise (Low calorie)

Method
Add the celery, mayonnaise, onion and tuna to a bowl and stir well. Spread the tuna mix onto the bagel, and top with the lettuce. Serve.

Nutrients per serving:
Protein: 25 g
Carbs: 32 g
Fat: 7 g
Cholesterol: 22 mg
Potassium: 320 mg
Sodium: 475 mg
Phosphorus: 175 mg

Dinner

Goulash
Serves: 6

Ingredients:
2 pounds beef round steak (Cubed)
1 tbsp wine vinegar
½ cup oil
2 tsp sweet paprika
1 ½ cups onion (Chopped)
1 cup low sodium beef stock
Flour or cornstarch
2 packages noodles (Cooked)

Method
Heat the oil in a pot, and brown the meat on both sides. Now add the onion, and sauté until the onion is almost clear. Add the stock and stir. Cover the pot, and then simmer for about 1 ½ hours. Once the allotted time is up, remove the meat from the pot, but keep it warm. Now add the paprika to the stock, and thicken it with the cornstarch or flour.

Add the wine vinegar, and stir. Divide the noodles between 6 plates, and spoon the goulash on top. Serve.

Nutrients per serving:
Protein: 37 g
Carbs: 10 g
Potassium: 700 mg
Sodium: 200 mg
Phosphorus: 300 mg

Day 15 of Healing Meal Plan

Breakfast

Zucchini Frittata
Serves: 4-5

Ingredients:
1/8 cup parsley (Chopped)
½ cup Bisquick mix
1 ½ cup zucchini (Grated)
2 eggs (Beaten)
½ onion (Chopped)
Pinch marjoram
½ garlic clove (Minced)
¼ cup Parmesan (Grated)
¼ cup canola oil

Method
Preheat your oven to 350 Fahrenheit, and add all of the ingredients to a bowl. Stir well, and pour the mixture into a greased baking pan. Bake for about 30 minutes, or until the frittata is a light brown and is set. Cut into 4-5 pieces, and serve.

Nutrients per serving:
Protein: 6 g
Carbs: 11 g
Fat: 18 g
Cholesterol: 98 mg
Potassium: 198 mg
Sodium: 260 mg
Phosphorus: 107 mg

Lunch

Pita Pizza
Serves: 2

Ingredients:
2 cloves garlic (Minced)
3 cup mozzarella
¼ cup onion (Chopped)
2 tbsp tomato sauce (Chunky)
¼ cup bell pepper (Chopped)
2 pita breads
2 ounces ground pork
½ tsp fennel seeds
¼ tsp red pepper flakes

Method
Preheat your oven to 400 Fahrenheit, and add the pork, bell pepper, onion, fennel, pepper flakes and garlic to a skillet, and sauté until the pork is cooked. Spray a baking sheet with a bit of cooking spray, and place the pita breads on top. Now add the meat and vegetable mix, and spread it on top of the pitas so the mix is evenly distributed.

Now take the tomato sauce, and spread it over the meat and vegetables. Sprinkle the cheese on top, and cook for about 5 minutes in the oven, or until the cheese starts to bubble.

Nutrients per serving:
Protein: 16 g
Carbs: 34 g
Fat: 10 g
Cholesterol: 138 mg
Potassium: 189 mg

Sodium: 381 mg
Phosphorus: 189 mg

Dinner

Crispy Lemon Chicken
Serves: 3-4

Ingredients:
2 cups white rice (Cooked)
1 tbsp parsley
½ pound chicken breast (Skinless, boneless, chopped into finger size)
3 lemon wedges
1 tsp herb seasoning blend
¼ cup lemon juice
1/8 tsp salt
1 tbsp olive oil
1/8 tsp black pepper
¼ cup all-purpose flour
1 small egg (Beaten)
1 tsp water

Method
Season the chicken with the seasoning blend, and then add the salt and pepper. Add the water and egg to a bowl, and stir well to combine. Place the flour in a different bowl. Now take the chicken and dip it in the egg mix, then dip it in the flour. Ensure the chicken is thoroughly coated.

Heat the oil in a pan, and sauté the chicken until it's nicely brown on all sides.

While the chicken cooks squeeze the lemon wedges onto it. Once the chicken is done, remove it from the pan, and blot it so that it doesn't go soggy. Divide the chicken between 4 plates, and then add the rice to the side. Garnish the chicken with the parsley and lemon wedges. Serve.

Nutrients per serving:
Protein: 22 g
Carbs: 39 g
Fat: 8 g
Cholesterol: 82 mg
Potassium: 234 mg
Sodium: 144 mg
Phosphorus: 201 mg

Day 16 of Healing Meal Plan

Breakfast

Lemon And Butter Muffins
Makes: 12

Ingredients:
2 cups all-purpose flour
1 cup blueberries
2 tsp baking powder
½ cup sugar
1 tsp lemon zest
½ cup soy milk
2 eggs (Beaten)
½ cup canola oil

Method
Preheat your oven to 375 Fahrenheit, and line a muffin tin with muffin cups. Add the baking powder, flour, and lemon zest to a bowl and whisk well. Now take another bowl and add the eggs, sugar, soy milk and canola oil, and whisk. Now make a well in the center of the bowl, and pour the egg mix along with the blueberries. Stir until everything is well combined and evenly distributed. Take a spoon and separate the batter between the cups in the muffin tin. Place the tin in the oven, and cook for about 18 minutes, or until the muffins are a golden brown. Remove, cool on a wire rack, and serve.

Nutrients per serving:
Protein: 3 g
Carbs: 21g
Fat: 10 g

Cholesterol: 35 g
Potassium: 47 mg
Sodium: 77 mg
Phosphorus: 116 mg

Lunch

__Chicken Sandwich With Orange Salad__
Serves: 3

Ingredients:
½ cup chicken (Cooked, chopped)
1 tbsp mayonnaise
1/8 cup onion (Chopped)
¼ cup green pepper (Chopped)
¼ cup celery (Sliced)
½ cup Mandarin oranges
3 bagels

Method
Add the onion, chicken, pepper, and celery to a bowl, and mix well. Now add the mayonnaise and oranges, mix again, but not too much. Spoon the salad mixture onto the bagels. Serve.

Nutrients per serving:
Protein: 7 g
Potassium: 146 mg
Sodium: 101 mg
Phosphorus: 59 mg

Dinner

Macaroni And Cheese
Serves: 4

Ingredients:
2 cups elbow pasta
¼ tsp black pepper
1 jar Pimento cheese spread (With cream cheese)
2 ounces green chilies (Diced)

Method
Cook the noodles as per the manufacturer's instructions (Do not add salt to the water). Add the cheese spread once the pasta is done. Stir well, and add the chilies. Serve with your choice of vegetables.

Nutrients per serving:
Protein: 6 g
Carbs: 25 g
Fat: 8 g
Cholesterol: 28 mg
Potassium: 83 mg
Sodium: 227 mg
Phosphorus: 74 mg

Day 17 of Healing Meal Plan

Breakfast

Bran & Raisin Oatmeal Breakfast Bar
Makes: 12

Ingredients:
1 cup oatmeal
1 cup water (Boiling)
½ cup whole wheat flour
3 tbsp brown sugar
1/3 cup raisins (Chopped)
1 ½ cups brans
1/3 cup corn oil

Method
Pour the water over the fruit, and allow the fruit to soak for about 20 minutes. Take the dry ingredients and add them to a large bowl. When the fruit has been soaked for 20 minutes, drain the liquid into a bowl and take 1 cup of the liquid out, and place it in a blender with the corn oil. Blend the oil and liquid for 1 minute, and then pour the oil mix into the same bowl as the dry ingredients, and mix together well. Add the fruit to the bowl, and mix again.

Now place the mixture into an oblong dish, and flatten the top down with a spatula or a large spoon. Make some markings on the batter so show where you're going to cut it when the breakfast bar is done. Place the dish in the oven, and cook for about 20-25 minutes at 375 Fahrenheit. Allow to cool, and then cut into slices, and refrigerate.

Nutrients per serving:
Protein: 2 g
Potassium: 142 mg
Sodium: A trace

Lunch

Oxtail Soup
Serves: 4

Ingredients:
½ bell pepper (Chopped)
6 ounces frozen vegetables
½ Jalapeño pepper (Chopped)
¼ tsp herb seasoning blend
½ onion (Diced)
Sprinkle black pepper
1 ½ celery stalks (Chopped)
1 tbsp vinegar
½ potato (Cubed)
1 pound oxtail
½ tbsp olive oil
1 bouillon cube
½ tbsp all purpose flour

Method
Add the olive oil, bouillon cube, and flour to a large pot. Fill the pot ¾ full with water, and then add the peppers. Allow to boil on a medium heat. Once boiling, add the vinegar and oxtail, and cover. Cook for 1 to 1 ½ hours, or until the oxtail is nice and tender.

Now add the seasoning blend, and black pepper. In a pan add the potatoes, and cook. Boil for about 6-8 minutes, and then drain. Add the celery, frozen vegetables, onion and potato to the pan again, and cook until the vegetables are done to your satisfaction. Serve.

Nutrients per serving:
Protein: 21 g
Carbs: 10 g
Fat: 21 g
Cholesterol: 66 mg
Potassium: 596 mg
Sodium: 325 mg
Phosphorus: 257 mg

Dinner

Shrimp & Pasta Salad
Serves: 4-5

Ingredients:
6 ounces pasta (Cooked)
1/3 cup olive oil
¼ red bell pepper (Diced)
¼ tsp garlic powder
½ yellow bell pepper (Diced)
½ tbsp Dijon mustard
¼ red onion (Diced)
¼ tsp black pepper
2 celery stalks (Diced)
1/8 cup balsamic vinegar
10 baby carrots (Chopped)
1/8 cup honey
¾ cup cauliflower (Chopped very small)
¼ pound salad shrimp (Cooked)
¼ English cucumber (Diced)

Method
Place all of the vegetables into a bowl, stir, and add the shrimp. In another bowl, add the black pepper, garlic powder, mustard and honey. Whisk well. Add the pasta to the vegetable bowl and mix well. Now pour the honey mixture over the pasta, and toss so the pasta is coated in the honey. Cover, and refrigerate for 5-6 hours. Stir well, and serve.

Nutrients per serving:
Protein: 16 g
Carbs: 65 g
Fat: 4 g
Potassium: 312 mg
Sodium: 143 mg
Phosphorus: 117 mg

Day 18 of Healing Meal Plan

Breakfast

Strawberry, Mango & Banana Salad
Serves: 4-5

Ingredients:
¼ tbsp lime zest
1 cup pineapple (Diced)
1/8 cup sugar
½ cup mango (Diced)
1/8 cup water
¾ cup strawberries (Sliced)
1/8 cup cilantro leave
1/3 cup banana (Sliced)

Method
Add the water to a saucepan, allow to boil, and then add the sugar. Let the water boil until the sugar is completely dissolved. Once the sugar has disappeared, remove the pan from the heat, and add the cilantro and lime, and allow to cool. Now add all of the fruit to a bowl, and stir well. Take a strainer, and strain the syrup, and remove any large lumps. Add the syrup to the fruit, stir well, and serve.

Nutrients per serving:
Protein: 2 g
Carbs: 18 g
Potassium: 160 mg
Sodium: 0
Phosphorus: 16 mg

Potato And Egg Sandwich
Serves: 4

Ingredients:
1 baking potato (Cooked, diced)
4 tsp salsa
2 tbsp canola oil
4 whole wheat sandwich thins
6 eggs (Beaten)

Method
Heat the oil in a skillet, and add the potatoes. Brown them, and drain off the oil. Place the potatoes back in the skillet, and then add the eggs. Stir for a few minutes, and then spoon the potato mix onto the sandwich thins. Top with the salsa, and serve.

Nutrients per serving:
Protein: 16 g
Carbs: 32 g
Fat: 15 g
Cholesterol: 279 mg
Potassium: 377 mg
Sodium: 318 mg
Phosphorus: 272 mg

Dinner

Beef Tibbs
Serves: 2

Ingredients:
1 onion (Sliced)
1/8 tsp black pepper
½ tomato (Chopped)
¼ tsp salt
½ green bell pepper (Chopped)
2 tbsp canola oil
8 ounces stewing beef (Lean, cubed)

Method
Add the onion to a skillet, and sauté until the onion is a little brown. Now add the tomato and beef, and allow to cook on a medium heat. Once the tomato and beef are half cooked, add the salt, bell pepper and pepper. Stir well, and cook for about 5-10 minutes, or until the beef is nice and tender. Serve with your choice of vegetables.

Nutrients per serving:
Protein: 25 g
Carbs: 6 g
Fat: 20 g
Cholesterol: 69 mg
Potassium: 503 mg
Sodium: 326 mg
Phosphorus: 230 mg

Day 19 of Healing Meal Plan

Breakfast

Maple Sausage
Makes: 15

Ingredients:
10 ounces maple sausage
½ cup onion (Minced)
20 ounces lean turkey (Ground)
1 tsp garlic powder
1 tsp poultry seasoning

Method
Add the turkey and sausage to a bowl and mix it together well. Add the rest of the ingredients, and mix again. Now using your hands, make patties that weigh approximately 2 ounces each. Add the patties to a skillet, and fry them on a medium heat for about 5 minutes, turn them over and fry on the other side for 3 more minutes. Serve.

Nutrients per serving (1 maple sausage):
Protein: 9 g
Carbs: 1 g
Potassium: 140 mg
Sodium: 49 mg
Phosphorus: 84 mg

Lunch

Pear And Pecan Salad

Serves: 4

Ingredients:
4 Asian pears (Cored, diced)
½ cup water
4 lettuce leaves
½ cup sugar
2 ounces blue cheese
½ cup pecans

Method
Add the sugar and water to a skillet, and heat on a low temperature until the sugar is dissolved. Add the pecans as quickly as you can, and stir well for about 20 seconds. Remove the pecans from the syrup, and place them onto some foil. Make sure you separate the pecans so they do not stick together.

Now take the lettuce leaves and place the pears on them. Add the cheese and pecans, and serve.

Nutrients per serving:
Protein: 6 g
Carbs: 41 g
Potassium: 297 mg
Sodium: 206 mg
Phosphorus: 127 mg

Dinner

Cranberry Chicken
Serves: 6

Ingredients:
1 tbsp olive oil
1 tbsp apple cider vinegar
½ cup onion (Chopped)
¼ cup brown sugar
2 pounds chicken breasts (Skinless, boneless)
16 ounces whole cranberries
¼ cup ketchup
1 tsp dry mustard

Method
Preheat the oil in a skillet, and add the onion. Sauté for a few minutes until the onion is clear. Add the chicken, and cook for about 4 minutes on both sides. In a bowl, add the mustard, brown sugar, ketchup, and vinegar. Stir until the ingredients have nicely combined. Pour the sauce into the skillet, and cover. Cook for about 20 minutes. Serve with your choice of vegetables.

Nutrients per serving:
Protein: 31 g
Carbs: 42 g
Fat: 6 g
Cholesterol: 85 mg
Potassium: 330 mg
Sodium: 248 mg
Phosphorus: 242 mg

Day 20 of Healing Meal Plan

Breakfast

Lemon And Apple Smoothie
Serves: 4

Ingredients:
¼ cup lemon juice
1 cup frozen vanilla yogurt
½ cup apple juice
2 tsp honey
1 apple (Cored, peeled)
1 banana

Method
Add all of the ingredients to a blender or smoothie maker, and blend well until smooth. Pour into a glass, and serve.

Nutrients per serving:
Protein: 2 g
Carbs: 38 g
Potassium: 327 mg
Sodium: 37 mg
Phosphorus: 59 mg

Lunch

Spicy Tenderloin Sandwich
Serves: 4

Ingredients:
1 ½ tbsp garlic paste
1 20 inch baguette

¾ tbsp granulated sugar
¼ cup mayonnaise (Fat free)
1 tsp herb seasoning blend
1 tbsp rice vinegar
1/8 tsp curry powder
1 Jalapeño pepper (Seeded, sliced)
½ pound pork tenderloin
½ cucumber (Sliced)
½ cup radishes (Shredded)
½ cup carrots (Shredded)
½ cup green onions

Method
Preheat your oven to 400 Fahrenheit, and add the sugar, seasoning, garlic paste and curry powder to a bowl. Mix well, and take ½ tbsp of the mix out, and set to one side. Take the remaining mix and spread it on the pork evenly.

Remove the thin end of the pork, and place it and the rest of the loin in a roasting pan & rack that's been sprayed with cooking spray. Place the pork in the oven for about 20 minutes. The thin end should only stay in for 10-12 minutes. Once the pork has been in the oven for the allotted times, cover it, and allow it to cool. Once the pork is cool place it in the refrigerator.

Add the radish, green onions, carrots, seasoning, sugar and rice vinegar to a bowl, and mix well. Set to one side. Now add the mayonnaise and the rest of the garlic paste to a bowl, stir and set to one side. Take the pork from the refrigerator, and slice it thinly.

Slice each baguette length-wise, and then take the mayonnaise mix and divide it into 2. Spread the mix onto each side of the baguette. Divide the carrot mix into 2 and spread it on the baguette. Now add the pork slices, Jalapeño, and cucumber on top. Place the 'lid' on the baguette, and cut it into 4. Serve.

Nutrients per serving:
Protein: 17 g
Carbs: 26 g
Fat: 5 g
Cholesterol: 40 mg
Potassium: 411 mg
Sodium: 374 mg
Phosphorus: 182 mg

Dinner

Apple Pork Chops With Stuffing
Serves: 6

Ingredients:
6 ounces chicken stuffing mix (Low sodium)
6 pork loin chops (Boneless)
2 tbsp margarine (Unsalted)
20 ounces apple pie filling

Method
Preheat your oven to 350 Fahrenheit. Spray a pan with some cooking spray. Now add the stuffing mix to a bowl and add the water and the water and margarine as per the manufacturer's instructions.

Now take the apple pie filling, and spread it along the bottom of the pan. Add the pork chops on top of the apple, and then spread the stuffing over the pork chops. Cover the pork with some foil, and add it to the oven. Bake for about 30 minutes, and then remove the foil. Place the pork chops back in the oven, and cook for another 10 minutes. Serve with your choice of vegetables.

Nutrients per serving:
Protein: 27 g
Carbs: 46 g
Fat: 22 g
Cholesterol: 57 mg
Potassium: 410 mg
Sodium: 365 mg
Phosphorus: 220 mg

Day 21 of Healing Meal Plan

Breakfast

French Toast With Baked Custard
Serves: 4

Ingredients:
4 slices bread (Preferably Italian)
4 cups un-enriched rice milk
2 cups egg substitute
1 tsp cinnamon
½ cup sugar
1 tsp almond extract
4 tbsp margarine (Unsalted, melted)

Method
Coat a baking pan with cooking spray, and ten place the slices of bread in the bottom of the pan so the pan base is covered. Add the egg, rice milk, margarine, almond, cinnamon, and sugar to a bowl, and beat together. Pour the egg mix over the bread. Cover the pan, and place in the refrigerator, and soak overnight. In the morning, remove from the refrigerator, and set the oven to 350 Fahrenheit. Place the baking pan in the oven, and bake for 40-45 minutes, or until a skewer that's been inserted into the middle of the French toast comes out clean. Serve.

Nutrients per serving:
Protein: 16 g
Carbs: 65 g
Fat: 14 g
Potassium: 221 mg
Sodium: 390 mg

Phosphorus: 111 mg

Lunch

Roasted Beets With Orange
Serves: 4-6

Ingredients:
1 bunch beets
½ tsp orange zest
1 tsp red wine vinegar
1 tsp olive oil

Method
Preheat your oven to 400 Fahrenheit, and then remove the tops of the beets. Wash them thoroughly, and wrap them quite loosely in some foil. Place the beets on a baking sheet, and roast for about 10-15 minutes, or until they are nice and tender. Once tender, remove the beets from the oven and allow to cool.
Once cooled, peel the beets, and top and tail them. The cut the beets into half. Take the vinegar and in a bowl add the beets and refrigerate them for one hour. Add the orange zest along with the olive oil, to the beets and allow them to soak for a few minutes. Serve right away.

Nutrients per serving:
Protein: 2 g
Carbs: 10 g
Potassium: 333 mg
Sodium: 80 mg
Phosphorus: 41 mg

Dinner

Eggplant & Crab Casserole
Serves: 4

Ingredients:
1 medium sized eggplant (Peeled, cubed)
1 tbsp melted butter
½ onion (Chopped)
¼ cup bread crumbs
½ bell pepper (Chopped)
¼ pound boiled shrimp
¼ cup celery (Chopped)
½ pound crab meat
1 clove garlic
2 eggs
1/8 cup olive oil
Small dash cayenne pepper
1/8 cup lemon juice
1/8 cup Parmesan
½ tbsp Worcestershire sauce
3 tbsp rice (Uncooked)
¼ tsp Tabasco saucepan
1/8 tsp creole seasoning

Method
Preheat your oven to 350 Fahrenheit. Place the eggplant into a saucepan and cover it with water. Boil until the eggplant becomes tender. This should take 5 minutes. Once the eggplant is done, drain the water, and set to one side. Now sauté the bell pepper, celery, garlic and onion, in the olive oil. Sauté until the vegetables are tender, but do not allow them to turn brown.

Now take the vegetables and add them to the eggplant, and fold in gently. Add the Worcestershire sauce, creole seasoning, rice, cheese, lemon juice, eggs, and cayenne pepper. Stir well, and then fold the crab and shrimp in.

Place the mixture into a casserole dish, and then take the bread crumbs and butter, and stir them together. Add the bread crumb mix onto the top of the casserole, spreading evenly. Add to the oven, and cook for about 30 minutes, or until the bread crumbs begin to turn brown. Serve.

<u>Nutrients per serving:</u>
Protein: 13 g
Carbs: 14 g
Fat: 12 g
Cholesterol: 138 mg
Potassium: 359 mg
Sodium: 229 mg
Phosphorus: 148 mg

Day 22 of Healing Meal Plan

Breakfast

Porridge
Serves: 2

Ingredients:
2 cups cracked wheat
1 cup cornmeal (Coarse)
1 cup oats
½ cup wheat bran
½ cup wheat germ (Toasted)
½ cup soy grits
½ cup wheat germ (Raw)
1 ¼ tsp salt

Method
Add the salt to a pan, and pour some water in, and bring to the boil. Once the water is boiling, slowly add each of the grains. Cook the grains for a few minutes while stirring now and again. Cover, and cook on a low heat for about 20 minutes, or until the porridge is cooked to your satisfaction. Serve.

Nutrients per serving:
Protein: 10 g
Carbs: 37 g
Potassium: 55 mg
Sodium: 2 mg
Phosphorus: 87 mg

Lunch

Chicken & Grape Salad
Serves: 4

Ingredients:
4 ounces pasta (Shell shape, cooked)
¾ cup mayonnaise
1 ½ cups chicken (Cooked, cubed)
8 ounces mandarin oranges
¾ cup celery (Chopped)
¾ cup seedless grapes (Sliced)

Method
Add all of the ingredients to a bowl and mix well. Cover, and place in the refrigerator for at least 30 minutes. Serve.

Nutrients per serving:
Protein: 17 g
Carbs: 31 g
Fat: 21 g
Cholesterol: 47 mg
Potassium: 291 mg
Sodium: 183 mg
Phosphorus: 159 mg

Dinner

Lamb Stew & Dumplings
Serves: 3-4

Ingredients:
3 cups water
½ tsp sugar

½ pound lamb stew meat (Trimmed, bitesize)
1 tsp baking powder
½ cup onion (Chopped)
¼ tsp salt
1 cup zucchini (Chopped)
1 cup all purpose white flour
1 ½ ounces green canned chilies

Method
Add the water to a stew pot, and then add the meat along with the bones to the water. Place on a medium heat, and then add the chilies, zucchini and onions. Allow the stew to boil, once it has just started boiling turn the heat down to low. Allow to simmer for an hour.

Take the baking powder, salt, sugar and flour, and add them to a mixing bowl. Stir well, and then need in a bit of warm water so you can form a ball. Cover the dough ball and allow to sit for 30 minutes. Once 30 minutes is up, remove up to 6 pieces that are the size of a penny. Cook the dumplings for 20 minutes in with the stew, and then serve.

Nutrients per serving:
Protein: 18 g
Carbs: 28 g
Fat: 12 g
Cholesterol: 55 mg
Potassium: 364 mg
Sodium: 357 mg
Phosphorus: 288 mg

Day 23 of Healing Meal Plan

Breakfast

Quick Omelet
Serves: 1

Ingredients:
2 eggs
½ cup your choice of meat or vegetables
2 tbsp water
1 tbsp margarine

Method
Add the eggs to a bowl along with the water and beat them well. Add the margarine to a skillet, and heat until the temperature is hot enough to evaporate a few drops of water. Add the egg mix, and let the edges of the omelet start to set, then turn it over and cook until the egg's nicely set. Now add your choice of meat or vegetables, and pour them onto one side of the omelet. Now fold the other side of the omelet over the meat or vegetables, and allow to cook for about 30 seconds. Remove the omelet from the heat, and serve.

Nutrients per serving:
Protein: 13 g
Carbs: 1.3 g
Potassium: 122 mg
Sodium: 296 mg
Phosphorus: 195 mg

Lunch

Red Pepper Soup

Serves: 6

Ingredients:
2 tbsp olive oil
½ cup cashews (Toasted)
6 garlic cloves (Minced)
1 tbsp red wine vinegar
1 tsp paprika
2/3 cup dry milk (Nonfat)
½ cup lentils (Rinsed)
2 cups chicken broth (Low sodium)
3 red peppers (Roasted)
28 ounces diced tomatoes

Method
Heat the oil in a pan, and add the onions. Sauté on a low heat for about 10 minutes, or until the onions are caramelized. Add the paprika and garlic, and cook for 2 more minutes. Now add the broth, lentils, tomatoes and peppers. Bring the pan to a boil, and then reduce the heat. Cover and allow to simmer for about 30 minutes, or until the lentils are soft.

Once the lentils are soft add the soup to a blender, and blend until smooth. Add the vinegar and dry milk, and stir well. Serve.

Nutrients per serving:
Protein: 11 g
Carbs: 31 g
Potassium: 370 mg
Sodium: 128 mg
Phosphorus: 83 mg

Dinner

Chicken Enchiladas
Serves: 6

Ingredients:
1 pound chicken (Ground)
1 can enchilada sauce
12 corn tortillas
½ cup onion (Chopped)

Method
Preheat your oven to 375 Fahrenheit, and then add the chicken to a skillet. Brown the chicken on a medium heat for about 10 minutes. And then add the cumin, garlic, pepper, and onion. Stir and cook until the onion has gone soft.
Add the tortillas to another skillet, and fry them in some oil. Once the tortillas are fried, dip them in some of the sauce.

Fill the tortillas with the meat, and place them back in the skillet for a few minutes. Remove from the skillet, and serve.

Nutrients per serving:

Protein: 13 g
Potassium: 222 mg
Sodium: 201 mg
Phosphorus: 146 mg

Day 24 of Healing Meal Plan

Breakfast

<u>Grilled Grapefruit With Honey</u>
Serves: 2

<u>Ingredients:</u>
1 grapefruit (Halved)
¼ tsp cinnamon
2 tsp honey

<u>Method</u>
Preheat your grill or broiler to 400 Fahrenheit. Take a knife and cut into the grapefruit sections so they are loose. Pour the honey over the grapefruit, dividing it equally between both halves. Sprinkle the cinnamon on each half, and then grill or broil for 4-6 minutes, or until the grapefruit has started to turn a little brown. Allow the grapefruit to cool for 1 minute, or longer if necessary, and serve.

<u>Nutrients per serving:</u>
Protein: 1 g
Carbs: 17 g
Fat: 0
Cholesterol: 0
Potassium: 174 mg
Sodium: 1 mg
Phosphorus: 13 mg

Lunch

<u>Tuna Burger And Egg Salad Sandwich</u>
Serves: 4

Ingredients:
7 ounces tuna (Low sodium)
4 lemon slices
¼ cup onion
4 pita breads
½ cup cilantro (Chopped)
¼ cup canola oil
1 tsp seasoning blend
1 tsp turmeric
1 clove garlic (Choppedo
5 eggs
½ tsp lemon pepper (No salt)

Method
Add all of the ingredients apart from the oil to a bowl.
Stir well, and then heat a skillet on a medium heat.
Add the tuna mix to the skillet, and turn it into a
patty. Fry until the patty is crispy and golden brown.
Make sure you turn it and cook the other side.

Now cut the patty into quarters, and place each
quarter inside a pita bread. Add a lemon wedge in
with the patty, and serve with the salad of your choice.

Nutrients per serving:
Protein: 27 g
Carbs: 34 g
Fat: 22 g
Cholesterol: 228 mg
Potassium: 280 mg
Sodium: 474 mg
Phosphorus: 250 mg

Dinner

Penne Pasta With Garlic & Asparagus
Serves: 6

Ingredients:
1 tbsp butter
¼ cup Parmesan (Shredded)
2 tbsp olive oil
8 ounces penne pasta (Wholewheat, cooked)
6 cloves garlic
½ tsp black pepper
1/8 tsp red pepper flakes
2 tsp lemon juice
1 pound asparagus (Sliced into 2 inch pieces)
½ tsp Tabasco

Method
Heat the oil and butter in a skillet on a medium heat.
Add the red pepper flakes and garlic, and sauté for 3
minutes. Now add the Tabasco, lemon juice,
asparagus and black pepper, and cook for about 5
minutes, or until the asparagus is tender.
Add the asparagus to the pasta and toss well. Sprinkle
the Parmesan on top, and serve.

Nutrients per serving:
Protein: 9 g
Carbs: 33 g
Fat: 10 g
Cholesterol: 13 mg
Potassium: 258 mg
Sodium: 93 mg
Phosphorus: 168 mg

Day 25 of Healing Meal Plan

Breakfast

Yogurt & Jell-O shake
Serves: 1

Ingredients:
¼ cup yogurt
¼ cup Jello-O (Already prepared)
¼ cup vanilla ice cream

Method
Add all of the ingredients to a blender or smoothie maker, and blend until smooth. Pour into a glass, and serve.

Nutrients per serving:
Protein: 5 g
Carbs: 21 g
Potassium: 209 mg
Sodium: 97 mg
Phosphorus: 137 mg

Lunch

Macaroni Salad
Serves: 8

Ingredients:
6 ounces macaroni (Cooked)
Pinch paprika
¼ cup onion (Chopped)
Pinch black pepper
¼ cup green peppers (Chopped)

½ tsp dry mustard
¼ cup celery (Chopped)
¼ cup mayonnaise
1/8 cup pimentos (Chopped)
2 small hard boiled eggs (Chopped)

Method
Add all of the ingredients apart from the black pepper and paprika to a bowl, and mix well. Now sprinkle the pepper and paprika on top, and refrigerate for at least 30 minutes. Serve.

Nutrients per serving:
Protein: 4 g
Carbs: 16 g
Fat: 7 g
Cholesterol: 42 mg
Potassium: 97 mg
Sodium: 78 mg
Phosphorus: 53 mg

Dinner

White Chili Chicken Crock Pot
Serves: 6

Ingredients:
½ cup Great Northern beans (Dried)
1 cup sour cream
½ cup black eye peas (Dried)
½ tsp cayenne pepper
½ cup lima beans (Dried)
½ tsp black pepper
¼ cup small lima beans (Dried)
1 tsp oregano
4 cups water

1 tsp cumin
1 pound chicken breasts (Cubed)
1 cup frozen corn
1 onion (Chopped)
1 tbsp canola oil
1 ½ tbsp garlic (minced)
1 Jalapeño pepper (Diced)

Method
Rinse the beans, and place them in your crock pot. Add the water, and turn the temperature to low. Now sauté the garlic, onions, chili peppers and chicken for about 10 minutes until the chicken is a little brown. Add these ingredients to the crock pot, and then add the spices and corn. Allow to cook for at least 9 hours. Stir well, and then add the sour cream. Stir again, and serve.

Nutrients per serving:
Protein: 25 g
Carbs: 32 g
Fat: 12 g
Potassium: 845 mg
Sodium: 75 mg
Phosphorus: 321 mg

Day 26 of Healing Meal Plan

Breakfast

Pumpkin & Apple Sauce Bread
Serves: 12

Ingredients:
1 ½ cups apple sauce (Unsweetened)
2 tsp pumpkin pie spice
1 cup brown sugar
½ tsp baking powder
2 cups all-purpose flour
½ cup vegetable oil
1 tsp baking soda
2 eggs

Method
Heat your oven to 350 Fahrenheit, and grease a loaf pan. Add the sugar, apple sauce, eggs, and oil to a bowl and whisk to combine. Take a separate bowl, and add the rest of the ingredients, and stir well.

Add the apple sauce mix to the flour mix and stir until they are just to combined. Now add the batter mix to the loaf pan, and place it on the oven. Bake for 50 minutes to 1 hour, or until a skewer that's been inserted into the center comes out clean. Allow to cool on a rack, and slice into 12 pieces. Serve.

Nutrients per serving (1 slice):
Protein: 3 g
Carbs: 38 g
Potassium: 82 mg
Sodium: 141 mg

Phosphorus: 41 mg

Lunch

Red Cabbage And Apple Salad
Serves: 6

Ingredients:
1 onion (Chopped)
1 red cabbage heat (Shredded)
1 tbsp salad oil
1 green apple (Cored, sliced)
¼ cup cider vinegar

Method
Add the onion to a skillet, and cook in oil until it;s soft. In a bowl add the pepper, sugar and vinegar. Stir well. Now add the apple and cabbage, and stir again. Add these ingredients to the skillet, and allow to boil. Reduce the heat and cover. Simmer for about 10 minutes, or until the cabbage is wilted. Serve.

Nutrients per serving:
Potassium: 157 mg
Sodium: 46 mg

Dinner

Cheese & Onion Perogies
Serves: 12

Ingredients:
3 potatoes (Peeled, sliced)
½ cup margarine
3 cups all-purpose flour

2 sweet onions (Sliced)
3 eggs
¾ cup sharp cheddar
¼ cup water

Method
Cook the potatoes in a pan and allow to boil. Once
they are boiling, drain the water away, and bring to
the boil with some fresh water. Allow to boil for 10
minutes and repeat. Stop cooking as soon as the
potatoes can be mashed.
Mash the potatoes, add the cheese and stir well. Set to
one side.

Add the flour to a bowl, and beat in the eggs. Now add
1 tbsp water, and make a dough. Add the dough to
stand for 10 minutes.

Divide the dough into 3 balls, and then roll one ball at
a time. You're aiming for a thickness about 1/8 of an
inch. Cut the dough into 12 squares, and then place
about 2 tbsp of the cheese mix into the center of the
squares.

Fold opposite edges of the squares together, and press
them down quite firmly to seal them. They place the
perogies on some waxed paper, and allow to sit for 1
hour. Add the onions to a skillet, and and sauté for
about 5 minutes. Sauté until the onions are soft.
Remove from the heat and set to one side.

Now boil a pot of water, and add 4 perogies to the pot.
Reduce the heat to a gentle boil, and cook until the
perogies start to float on the surface. Once they are
done, remove them from the pot, and add the next
batch. Repeat a third time, and then add the perogies

to a plate. Sprinkle the onions over the top, and cook on a low heat until the perogies have started to go a golden color. Serve.

Nutrients per serving (3 perogies):
Protein: 8 g
Carbs: 32 g
Fat: 12 g
Cholesterol: 60 mg
Potassium: 176 mg
Sodium: 128 mg
Phosphorus: 120 mg

Day 27 of Healing Meal Plan

Breakfast

Breakfast Sausage And Egg Casserole
Serves: 8-10

Ingredients:
8 ounces pork sausage (Low fat)
½ tsp onion flakes (Dried)
8 ounces cream cheese
½ tsp mustard (Dry)
1 cup low fat milk
5 eggs
4 slices white bread (Cubed)

Method
Preheat your oven to 325 Fahrenheit. Take a skillet, and crumble the sausages into it. Cook until the sausages are just done. And then set to one side. Place all of the other ingredients apart from the bread into a blender. Blend until smooth, then add the sausages, and blend again.

Take a casserole dish, and add the bread to the bottom of the dish. Pour the sausage mix over the bread, and place the dish in the oven. Cook for about 50 minutes, or until the mixture is set. Slice into 8-10 portions, and serve.

Nutrients per serving:
Protein: 11 g
Carbs: 9 g
Fat: 16 g
Cholesterol: 149 mg

Potassium: 201 mg
Sodium: 356 mg
Phosphorus: 159 mg

Lunch

<u>Vegetarian Pizza</u>
Serves: 8

<u>Ingredients:</u>
½ cup red onion (Diced)
Pizza base
½ cup green bell pepper (Chopped)
1 cup red pepper and tomato sauce
½ cup mushroom (Chopped)
2 tbsp Parmesan (Shredded)
½ cup pineapple tidbits
½ cup Mozzarella (Shredded)

<u>Method</u>
Spread the tomato sauce over the pizza base, and add the mushroom, bell pepper, onion, and pineapple. Now sprinkle the cheese on top, and bake in the oven for about 12 minutes, or until the pizza is starting to brown at the edges. Serve.

<u>Nutrients per serving:</u>
Protein: 8 g
Carbs: 37 g
Fat: 12 g
Cholesterol: 5 mg
Potassium: 210 mg
Sodium: 165 mg
Phosphorus: 111 mg

Dinner

Roast Chicken With Herbs & Lemon
Serves 4

Ingredients:
4 pound chicken
1 tbsp olive oil
1 lemon (Sliced)
2 tbsp butter (Unsalted, softened)
2 ½ tbsp thyme and sage
1 garlic cloves (Peeled, crushed)

Method
Preheat your oven to 450 Fahrenheit, and add the chicken to a roasting pan. Now add the garlic, herbs and butter to a bowl and mix well. Add the butter to the inside of the chicken, and place the lemon in there too.

Take the olive oil, and rub it into the chicken skin. Add to the oven, and roast the chicken for approximately 1 hour. Once the chicken is done, drain the juices, and pour them over the chicken, along with the lemon slices.

Let the chicken stand for about 20 minutes, carve and serve.

Nutrients per serving (3 ounces):
Protein: 19 g
Carbs: 0 g
Fat: 0 g
Potassium: 222 mg
Sodium: 77 mg
Phosphorus: 188 mg

Day 28 of Healing Meal Plan

Breakfast

<u>Wheat Berry & Ginger Cereal</u>
Serves: 4

<u>Ingredients:</u>
½ cup wheat berries (Cooked)
½ tsp cinnamon
1 pear (Thinly sliced)
2 tbsp maple syrup
2 tbsp crystallized ginger (Chopped)
1 tbsp butter
1 tsp orange zest
½ cup cranberries (Fresh)

<u>Method</u>
Add the butter to a pan on a medium to low heat, and let it melt. Add the pear, and cook it until the pear has just turned tender. Now add the ginger and cranberries, and cook until the cranberries start to open up. Once the cranberries are opening, add the cinnamon, wheat berries, maple syrup and orange zest. Stir, and allow the ingredients to heat through. Serve.

<u>Nutrients per serving:</u>
Protein: 3 g
Carbs: 36 g
Fat: 2 g
Cholesterol: 5 mg
Potassium: 220 mg
Sodium: 19 mg
Phosphorus: 90 mg

Lunch

Roasted Cauliflower With Paprika
Serves: 6

Ingredients:
1 head cauliflower (Chopped)
½ lemon (Juiced)
¼ cup olive oil
1 tsp paprika

Method
Preheat your oven to 400 Fahrenheit. Add the cauliflower, pepper, lemon juice and paprika to a bowl. Toss to ensure the cauliflower is coated in the mixture.

Now add the cauliflower to a roasting pan, and cook in the oven for about 20 minutes, or until the cauliflower starts to turn a little brown. Stir once, and serve.

Nutrients per serving:
Protein: 4 g
Carbs: 12 g
Potassium: 356 mg
Sodium: 63 mg
Phosphorus: 95 mg

Dinner

Microwave Salmon Steaks
Serves: 4

Ingredients:
3 tbsp butter
4 lemon wedges
4 salmon steaks (6 ounces each)
1 tsp paprika
1 ½ tsp lemon juice
1 tsp tarragon
½ tsp lemon pepper
2 lemon slices (Halved)
½ tsp garlic powder
4 onion slices
½ tsp onion powder

Method
Grease a baking dish with 1 tbsp butter, and add the salmon. Sprinkle the salmon with the garlic powder, lemon juice, onion powder, and lemon pepper. Now add 1 piece of lemon, and 1 slice of onion to each steak. Sprinkle with paprika and tarragon.

Now cover the dish with some plastic wrap, and microwave on a high heat for about 5 minutes, or until the salmon is done. Serve with the lemon wedges and your choice of vegetables.

Nutrients per serving:
Protein: 42 g
Potassium: 400 mg
Sodium: 250 mg
Phosphorus: 450 mg

Day 29 of Healing Meal Plan

Breakfast

Lemon And Blueberry Muffins
Serves: 12

Ingredients:
¾ cup yellow cornmeal
1 cup blueberries
¾ cup whole wheat flour
1 tsp lemon zest
1 ½ tsp baking powder
2 tbsp lemon juice
¼ cup sugar
1 egg (Beaten)
¾ cup milk
2 tbsp margarine

Method
Preheat your oven to 400 Fahrenheit, and then spray a muffin pan with cooking spray. Add the cornmeal, sugar, baking powder, and flour to a bowl, and stir to combine. In another bowl add the margarine, lemon juice, oil, lemon zest, and milk. Now stir the milk mixture into the cornmeal mixture, but don't over stir, stop when the two mixtures have only just combined.

Add the blueberries and stir just a little more to combine them.

Pour the mix into the muffin pan, and place it into the oven. Cook for about 25 minutes, or until a skewer that's been inserted into the center of the muffins comes out clean. Allow to cool on a rack, and serve.

Nutrients per serving (1 muffin):
Protein: 3 g
Carbs: 19 g
Fat: 2 g
Potassium: 92 mg
Sodium: 76 mg
Phosphorus: 71 mg

Lunch

Basil & Pineapple Salad
Serves: 5

Ingredients:
4 cups pineapple (Cubed)
½ cup blueberries
3 cups strawberries (Quartered)
1 tbsp lime zest
½ cup sweetener
½ cup cilantro (Chopped)

Method
Add the sweetener to a pan, along with about ½ cup water. Allow to boil and cook for 1 minute. Now take the pan off the heat, and add the lime zest and basil. Stir well. Allow the mixture to cool to room temperature, then strain, throwing away the solids.

Add the blueberries, strawberries and pineapple to a bow, and mix well. Add the sweetener, and stir well to ensure the fruit is coated. Place in the refrigerator for at least 30 minutes, and serve.

Protein: 1g
Carbs: 12 g
Fat: 0 g
Cholesterol: 0 g
Potassium: 148 mg
Sodium: 2 mg
Phosphorus: 18 mg

Dinner

Zucchini & Mushroom Lasagna
Serves: 8

Ingredients:
8 ounces cream cheese (Whipped)
8 lasagna noodles
1 Roma tomato (Diced)
4 tbsp olive oil
½ cup Portabella mushrooms (Chopped)
1 tbsp oregano
½ cup zucchini (Sliced)
1 tbsp basil
½ cup kale (Chopped)
1 tsp garlic (Crushed)
1 pound ground beef
½ cup Parmesan (Shredded)
2 eggs

Method
Preheat your oven to 375 Fahrenheit. Add the beef to a skillet, and brown. Set to one side. Now add the Parmesan, cream cheese, ½ cup water and 1 egg to a bowl and stir well. Take another bowl, and add the basil, garlic, oregano, 1 egg, beef, and ¼ water. Stir well. Add 3 tbsp olive oil, and stir well.

Sauté the kale and mushrooms with the rest of the olive oil. Add ¼ of the beef to a pan, and spread evenly. Add 4 lasagna noodles, and ½ the cream cheese. Add the zucchini, kale and mushrooms, and the ground beef in layers, and repeat until you have some cream cheese at the top. Add the tomato, and place the pan in the oven, covered with foil. Cook for 30 minutes, remove the foil, and cook for another 10 minutes. Remove the lasagna from the oven, and allow to stand for 10 minutes. Serve.

Nutrients per serving:
Protein: 25 g
Carbs: 45 g
Fat: 23 g
Cholesterol: 100 mg
Potassium: 492 mg
Sodium: 214 mg
Phosphorus: 242 mg

Day 30 of Healing Meal Plan

Breakfast

Egg Bake
Serves: 6

Ingredients:
3 slices English muffin bread
¼ tsp cilantro
6 eggs
¼ tsp rosemary
1 cup rice milk (Unflavored)
1 tsp oregano
½ cup Mozzarella (Shredded)
1 tsp ground mustard
¼ cup mushrooms (Chopped)
½ tsp black pepper
¼ cup onion (Diced)
Pinch salt
¼ cup red bell pepper (Chopped)
1 tsp garlic (Minced)

Method
Add the English muffins to a baking dish, and crumble them. In a bowl, add the rice milk, and eggs, beat together well, and add the rest of the ingredients to the bowl too. Stir well to combine, and then pour the egg mix over the muffins. Stir well. Cover the baking dish with plastic wrapping, and place in the refrigerator for at least 8 hours. Once the allotted time is up, preheat your oven to 350 Fahrenheit. Take the plastic wrap off the baking dish, and place the egg bake in the oven. Cook for about 1 hour, or until the eggs are done to your satisfaction. Serve.

Nutrients per serving:
Protein: 11 g
Carbs: 17 g
Fat: 7 g
Cholesterol: 218 mg
Potassium: 147 mg
Sodium: 343 mg
Phosphorus: 187 mg

Lunch

Zucchini Provençal
Serves: 6

Ingredients:
5 zucchini (Chopped)
2 red bell peppers
2 potatoes (Chopped)
2 tomatoes (Chopped)
1 cup celery (Diced)
2 tbsp oil
½ cup green onions (Diced)
½ tsp cilantro

Method
Add the basil, celery, onions and oil to a pan, and sauté them until the onions are starting to turn translucent (This should take about 5 minutes). Add the rest of the ingredients, stir well, and cover. Steam the Provençal for 5 minutes, or until the zucchini is tender. Serve.

Nutrients per serving:
Protein: 4 g

Carbs: 21 g
Potassium: 988 mg
Sodium: 38 mg
Phosphorus: 131 mg

Dinner

<u>Chicken Squares</u>
Serves: 8

<u>Ingredients:</u>
1 ½ pound chicken breast (Cooked, boneless, skinless)
2 packages crescent rolls (Original)
6 ounces cream cheese (Softened)
1 cup broccoli florets (Chopped, cooked)
2 tbsp margarine (Unsalted)

<u>Method</u>
Preheat your oven to 350 Fahrenheit. Add the chicken and cream cheese to a bowl, mix well, and then add the broccoli and margarine, mix again. Take the crescent rolls, and make 2 rectangles with the dough. Spoon about 1/8 the chicken mix into the center of each rectangle. Now wrap the dough around the mixture, and then fold the edges so that it seals.

Place the rectangles on a baking tray, and add to the oven. Bake for about 30 minutes, or until the chicken squares are a nice golden brown. Serve.

<u>Nutrients per serving:</u>
Protein: 18 g
Carbs: 24 g
Fat: 24 g
Cholesterol: 56 mg

Potassium: 224 mg
Sodium: 539 mg
Phosphorus: 176 mg

Conclusion and Tips

If you would like to take part in the diet, you may appreciate a few helpful tips:

Make a note of any changes in your symptoms

Once you have been on the renal diet for a few weeks, you should start to see a change in any symptoms you experience. You may not see a huge change, but there may be a few noticeable ones. A great way for you to stay motivated is to make a note of these positive changes, and of course, speak to your doctor about them.

Write down your favorite recipes

Another great way for you to stay motivated is to write down, or print out a copy of your favorite recipes. This could encourage you to eat them a little more often, which could also help you to stay healthy. Please don't forget to monitor your potassium, phosphorus, and sodium levels daily. If one of your favorite meals contains a lot of potassium for example, you may need to restrict how many times you eat it.

The renal diet can help you to reduce symptoms associated with kidney disease, or it can simply prevent it from getting any worse. If you're thinking of taking up this diet, please speak to your doctor. Many people suffer from kidney disease, and although this book gives a general overview as to how you can help reduce symptoms, it cannot work on a personal level. If you need to dramatically reduce your phosphorus intake, you may need to alter the recipes contain in this book, so they are more suited to your needs.

Let the renal diet improve your symptoms while also helping you to lower your blood pressure, work on your diabetes, while you enjoy some healthy meals that can do you the world of good.

If you are concerned about any of your symptoms, or you're worried that you may develop kidney disease, please speak to your doctor.

Thank You

Before you go, we would like to say a warm "THANK YOU" on behalf of the Vigor & Belle family! We started this brand to help our customers live healthier, more vibrant lives and we hope that this book has served you in many ways.

If you enjoyed this book, then we'd like to ask you for a favor!

Please take a moment and leave a review for this book after you turn the page.

This feedback is crucial for us to continue to help you to live a healthier, happier and more vibrant lifestyle! If you loved this book, we would love to hear from you!

Live Healthy & Stay Beautiful,

The vigor&belle Family

55081331R00068

Made in the USA
Lexington, KY
10 September 2016